P9-CMD-864

Read-About® Health

Fats, Oils, and Sweets

By Carol Parenzan Smalley

Consultants

Reading Adviser
Nanci R. Vargus, EdD
Assistant Professor of Literacy
University of Indianapolis, Indianapolis, Indiana

Subject Adviser
Janet M. Gilchrist, PhD, RD
Nutritionist

Children's Press®
A Division of Scholastic Inc.
New York   Toronto   London   Auckland   Sydney
Mexico City   New Delhi   Hong Kong
Danbury, Connecticut

Designer: Herman Adler Design
Photo Researcher: Caroline Anderson
The photo on the cover shows different sources of fats, oils, and sweets.

Library of Congress Cataloging-in-Publication Data

Smalley, Carol Parenzan, 1960–
  Fats, oils, and sweets / by Carol Parenzan Smalley.
      p. cm. — (Rookie read-about health)
  Includes index.
  ISBN 0-516-25289-5 (lib. bdg.)   0-516-24759-X (pbk.)
  1. Oils and fats—Juvenile literature. 2. Nutrition—Juvenile literature.
3. Confectionery—Juvenile literature. I. Title. II. Series.
  TX560.F3S62 2005
  613.2'84—dc22   C   2005004775

CHILDREN'S PRESS, and ROOKIE READ-ABOUT®,
and associated logos are trademarks and/or registered trademarks
of Scholastic Library Publishing. SCHOLASTIC and associated logos
are trademarks and/or registered trademarks of Scholastic Inc.

1 2 3 4 5 6 7 8 9 10 R 14 13 12 11 10 09 08 07 06 05

Many kids like candy, cake, cookies, and soft drinks.

But be careful how often you enjoy these treats!

Fruits and vegetables can be just as tasty. So can certain grains and low-fat dairy foods.

Candy, cake, cookies,
and soft drinks belong to
the fats, oils, and sweets
food group.

How often should you eat
foods from this group?

Scientists can help you answer this question. They came up with the Food Guidance System. It explains how often people should eat different foods to stay healthy.

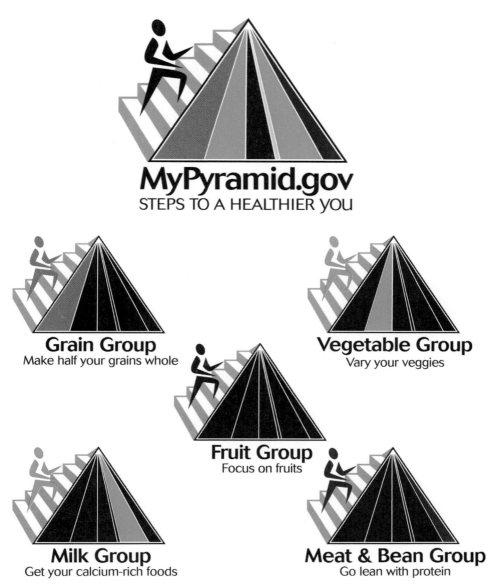

MyPyramid.gov
STEPS TO A HEALTHIER YOU

Grain Group
Make half your grains whole

Vegetable Group
Vary your veggies

Fruit Group
Focus on fruits

Milk Group
Get your calcium-rich foods

Meat & Bean Group
Go lean with protein

9

You should only eat fats, oils, and sweets once in a while.

These foods aren't always bad for you. But most have very few vitamins or minerals.

Vitamins and minerals are nutrients. You need nutrients to stay healthy.

Too many sweets can cause tooth problems such as cavities. They can also cause people to be overweight.

14

It's important to eat foods from all the groups.

People who eat too many sweets often forget to do this. When this happens, they don't get enough nutrients.

But fats aren't always bad. They add flavor to food and give you energy.

Butter, sour cream, salad dressing, and gravy all have fat.

17

18

Oils are made from plant seeds. Some oils are good for you.

Olive, canola, soy, corn, sunflower, and peanut oils are healthy.

Certain oils are not good for you. Coconut and palm oils are unhealthy.

These oils are sometimes used to make cookies and crackers.

Sugar often comes from sugarcane plants.

Sweets are usually made with sugar. The sugar we eat comes from the plants sugarcane or beet cane.

Honey, fruit juice, maple syrup, and corn syrup are also used to make sweets.

Today, people eat about 150 pounds of sugar each year. That's a lot of sugar.

It's the same weight as three average seven-year-old children!

Limit the fats, oils, and sweets you eat.

Be sure to eat plenty of low-fat foods from the other food groups.

And don't forget to exercise! All these steps will help you stay healthy.

Words You Know

butter

cake

candy

cookies

exercise

oils

soft drink

sugarcane

Index

About the Author

Carol Parenzan Smalley grew up smelling chocolate every day. She was born and raised in Hershey, Pennsylvania. Today, Carol, her husband, daughter, and 18-year-old cat live in a log cabin in the Adirondack Mountains of New York. Her favorite sweet treats are licorice and hot chocolate with lots of marshmallows.

Photo Credits

Photographs © 2005: Corbis Images: 17 bottom right (Owen Franken), 26 (John and Lisa Merrill), 29, 31 top left (Tim Pannell), 6 bottom right, 31 bottom left (Lew Robertson), 6 top right, 25 top left, 25 top right, 30 top right (Royalty-Free); Envision Stock Photography Inc.: 17 top left, 30 top left (MAK Studio), 18, 31 top right (Steven Mark Needman); Getty Images: 17 bottom left (Comstock Images), 21 (Andrew McCaul/The Image Bank); PhotoEdit: cover (Amy Etra), 14 (Spencer Grant), 22, 31 bottom right (Betts Anderson Loman), 6 bottom left, 10, 13, 25 bottom left, 30 bottom right (Michael Newman), 5, 6 top left, 17 top right, 30 bottom left (Jonathan Nourok), 25 bottom right (David Young-Wolff); Stone/Getty Images/Christel Rosenfeld: 3.